Colors of Horses

written by
Mona Brand

illustrated by
Karen Maizel

KAEDEN BOOKS™

Table of Contents

Brown 4

Black 5

White 6

Gray 7

Red or Blue. 8

Gold 10

Spots or Stripes. 12

Glossary. 15

Index 16

Brown

Horses can be many colors.
There are brown horses.

4

Black

There are black horses.

White

There are white horses.

Gray

There are gray horses.

Red or Blue

Horses can be red or blue.

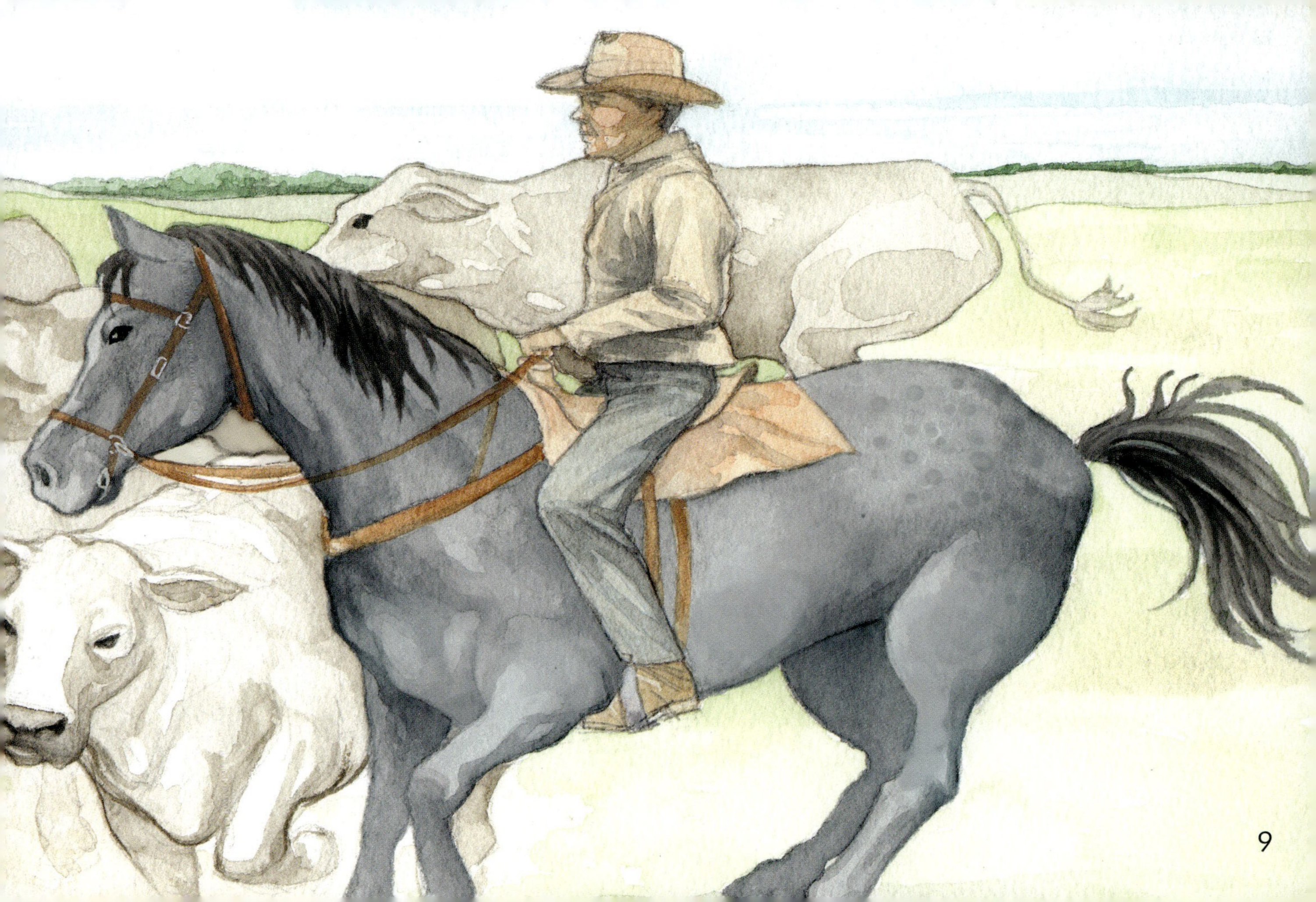

Gold

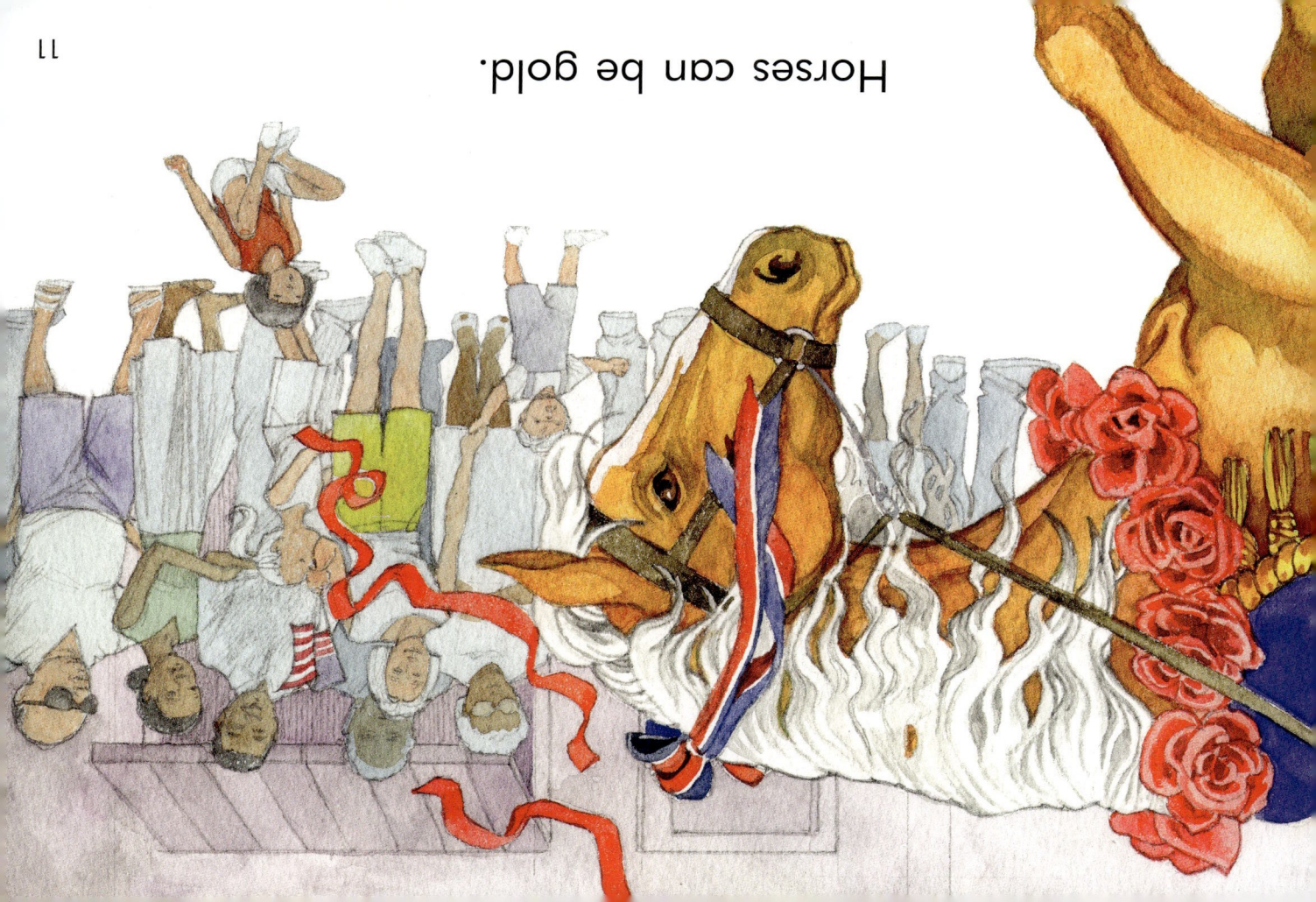

Horses can be gold.

Spots or Stripes

There are horses with **spots**.

There are horses with stripes.

Quarter Horse | **Thoroughbred** | Lippizan | Percheron

Red and Blue Roans | **Palomino** | Paint | Buckskin

Which horse do you like?

Glossary

horses – large animals that are used for riding, carrying, or pulling things

Palomino – a kind of horse with a golden coat and a white mane and tail

spots – small, round marks or stains

Thoroughbred – a kind of horse used in horse racing

Index

black 5

blue 8

brown 4

gold 10, 11

gray 7

red 8

white 6